NOV   2012

SOLAR POWER

Chris Oxlade

Heinemann LIBRARY

Chicago, Illinois

www.heinemannraintree.com
Visit our website to find out
more information about
Heinemann-Raintree books.

To order:

☎ Phone 888-454-2279

💻 Visit www.heinemannraintree.com
to browse our catalog and order online.

Edited by Louise Galpine and Laura Knowles
Designed by Philippa Jenkins
Illustrations by KJA-artists.com
Original illustrations © Capstone Global Library
    Limited 2012
Illustrated by KJA-artists.com
Picture research by Mica Brancic
Originated by Capstone Global Library Limited
Printed and bound in China by CTPS

15 14 13 12 11
10 9 8 7 6 5 4 3 2 1

Library of Congress Cataloging-in-Publication Data
Cataloging-in-Publication data is available at the Library
of Congress.

ISBN 978 1 4329 5445 1(hardback)
ISBN 978 1 4329 5459 8(paperback)

Acknowledgments
We would like to thank the following for permission to
reproduce photographs: Alamy pp. **5** (© David Burton),
12 (© Alan Skyrme), **22** (© Idealink Photography);
Corbis pp. **4** (Science Faction/© NASA—digital version
copyright), **7** (© Bettmann), **8** (© Kevin Fleming), **10**
(© Michael Nicholson), **20** (© Grafton Marshall Smith),
21 (Science Faction/© Hank Morgan—Rainbow), **23**
(Reuters), **24** (© Bettmann); Getty Images pp. **15**
(Popperfoto), **17** (Time & Life Pictures/Life Magazine/
Ralph Crane), **19** (Science & Society Picture Library),
27 (AFP Photo/Martin Sylvest/Scanpix Denmark);
Naval Research Laboratory p. **18**; © PlanetSolar p. **25**;
Shutterstock p. **9** (© Rob Byron); TopFoto.co.uk p. **26**
(Geoff Caddick).

Cover photograph of a man cooking by Sun's rays on a
solar cooker, c. 1950–1959, reproduced with permission
of Getty Images /© Time & Life Pictures/Carl Iwasaki.

We would like to thank Peter Smithurst for his
invaluable help in the preparation of this book.

Every effort has been made to contact copyright holders
of material reproduced in this book. Any omissions will
be rectified in subsequent printings if notice is given to
the publisher.

CONTENTS

Look for these boxes

Biographies

These boxes tell you about the life of inventors, the dates when they lived, and their important discoveries.

Setbacks

Here we tell you about the experiments that didn't work, the failures, and the accidents.

EUREKA!

These boxes tell you about important events and discoveries, and what inspired them.

Any words appearing in the text in bold, **like this**, are explained in the glossary.

TIMELINE

2011—The timeline shows you when important discoveries and inventions were made.

WHAT IS SOLAR POWER?

The word "solar" means "relating to the Sun." "Solar power" means using the energy in the Sun's rays (solar energy) to create electricity and heat. Before we can produce solar power, we have to catch solar energy somehow—and that is where solar-power inventions come in. They include simple ancient inventions, such as rooms warmed by solar energy, and complex modern inventions, such as **solar power stations**.

Light and heat

We use solar energy in two different ways. The first is to heat water and buildings. This is known as **solar thermal** power. The second is to produce electricity. This is known as solar voltaic power.

Earth is flooded with sunlight, a limitless source of energy.

Around 400 BCE—From Greek writings, we know that the ancient Greeks built solar-heated houses (see page 6)

200 BCE—The Greek scientist Archimedes may have sunk a Roman fleet using sunlight and mirrors (see page 7)

Importance of solar energy

Most scientists believe that the main cause of **global warming** (the gradual warming of Earth) is the carbon dioxide gas that is released into the air when we burn **fossil fuels**, such as coal or oil. Solar power does not produce carbon dioxide. It is an **environmentally friendly** form of power. It is also a **renewable energy**, meaning it can be used again and again. Solar energy will keep coming from the Sun for billions of years.

Solar power is only possible because of the enormous power of the Sun. The Sun began to shine more than four billion years ago. Earth and other planets formed soon after. Without the Sun's energy, life on Earth would be impossible. The Sun warms Earth, and plants use sunlight to grow.

With the help of **solar cells**, energy from the Sun can be used to charge a cell phone.

CATCHING THE SUN

The first sort of solar power technology was very simple. Today, we call it passive solar power. This is letting the Sun's rays shine into a building to warm up the rooms. The rays warm the walls, floor, and objects in the room, and in turn these warm the air in the room.

In countries in the **northern hemisphere**, the Sun is in the south in the middle of the day. The ancient Greeks built their houses with windows facing south, so that the Sun would shine in during cool winter days.

Roman sun rooms

The ancient Romans also built rooms with south-facing windows for winter living. The rooms were called *heliocaminus* (sun furnaces). The windows were covered with sheets of a see-through mineral called *mica* to stop the heat from escaping.

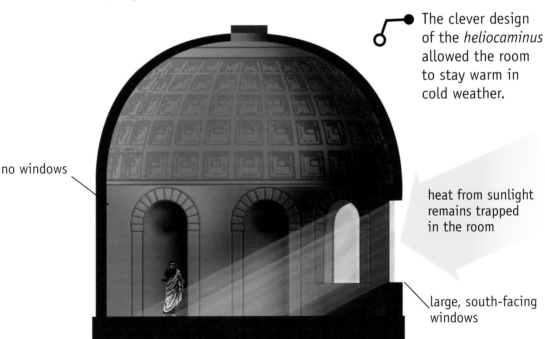

The clever design of the *heliocaminus* allowed the room to stay warm in cold weather.

no windows

heat from sunlight remains trapped in the room

large, south-facing windows

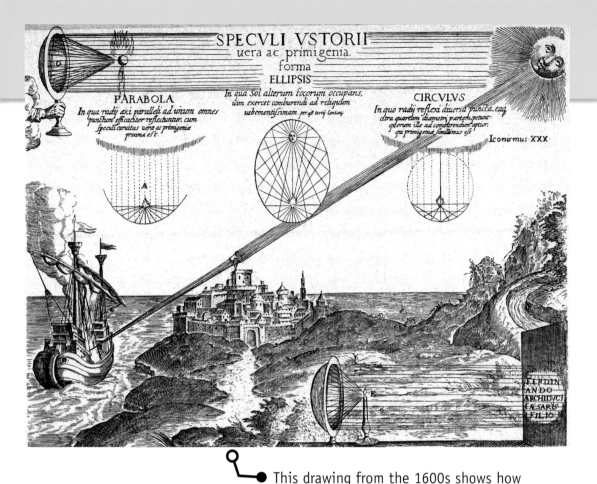

This drawing from the 1600s shows how Archimedes might have used the Sun's power to set Roman ships on fire and sink them.

EUREKA!

For more than 2,500 years, people have used mirrors to direct the Sun's rays to start a fire. There is a story that in around 200 BCE, the Greek scientist Archimedes set fire to a fleet of Roman warships using sunlight bounced off bronze shields.

1200—The Pueblo people build solar-heated terraced houses in Acoma, New Mexico (see page 8)

1700—"Saltbox" houses are built by settlers in New England (see page 9)

Solar settlements

Some of the native peoples of North America also captured the Sun's energy to keep warm. An example comes from around 800 years ago, in what is now Acoma, New Mexico. The Pueblo people built stone-and-mud houses in streets lined up east to west. This meant the fronts of the houses faced to the south. The houses also had two or three stories, each with a south-facing terrace (outside area for sitting). This arrangement meant that the houses captured as much sunshine as possible, especially during cold winters.

The ancient town of Acoma is a famous Pueblo settlement. It was built around 800 years ago.

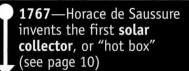

1767—Horace de Saussure invents the first **solar collector**, or "hot box" (see page 10)

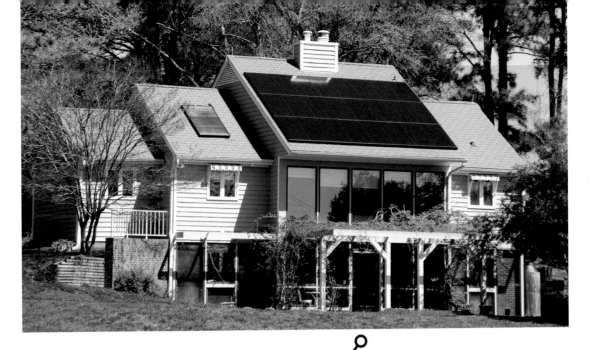

This modern house has large windows to capture the Sun's rays.

Big windows

People in northern Europe began using solar power in the 1700s. Large country houses had big rooms that were hard to heat with open fires. So the rooms were built with large windows to let in warming sunshine.

At the same time, people started to build greenhouses. These trap lots of solar energy. They were sometimes attached to the south wall of a house, so that the heat trapped inside helped to heat the house. Greenhouses were also built to grow tropical plants in cool **climates**. They became very popular in the 1800s. Many modern buildings are designed to capture solar energy in a similar way, using large windows.

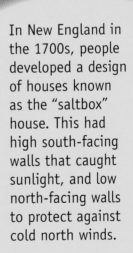

EUREKA!

In New England in the 1700s, people developed a design of houses known as the "saltbox" house. This had high south-facing walls that caught sunlight, and low north-facing walls to protect against cold north winds.

9

HEATING WITH THE SUN

A **solar collector** catches solar energy for cooking, or to heat water for showers, baths, and washing. The first solar collector we know about was invented by Swiss scientist Horace de Saussure in 1767. It was simply a box, lined with black cork and covered with a glass lid.

The lining of the box was black because black things **absorb** (soak up) heat well. In sunlight, the lining got hot and heated the air inside the box, and the glass lid stopped the heat from escaping. In hot sunshine, the temperature inside rose to an amazing 228 °Celsius (442 °Fahrenheit). That is hot enough to boil a cup of water placed in the box. Modern solar ovens (see page 27), which use solar energy to cook food, work in the same way.

Horace de Saussure (1740–1799) invented a solar oven, as well as a device to measure air **humidity**.

1800s—Sun rooms and greenhouses become increasingly popular in northern Europe (see page 9)

Water heaters

The first solar collectors for heating water appeared in the 1890s. They were simply metal water tanks painted black on the outside. The Sun heated the tank itself, and the tank heated the water inside. The first solar water heater people could buy was the Climax Solar Water Heater, invented by American Clarence Kemp in 1891.

Price of No. 1 Heater for 1892 Reduced to $15 Net

Climax Solar-Water Heater

UTILISING ONE OF NATURE'S GENEROUS FORCES

THE SUN'S HEAT {Stored up in Hot Water for Baths, Domestic and other Purposes

GIVES HOT WATER at all HOURS OF THE DAY AND NIGHT.

NO DELAY.

FLOWE INSTANTLY.

NO CARE — NO WORRY.

ALWAYS CHARGED

ALWAYS READY

THE WATER AT TIMES ALMOST BOILS.

Price, No. 1, $25.00

This Size will Supply sufficient for 3 to 8 Baths

CLARENCE M. KEMP, BALTIMORE, MD.

OUTLET   INLET

This is an advertisement for one of the first solar water heaters people could buy for their homes.

Setbacks

Clarence Kemp's invention was a great success. By 1900 one in three homes in the city of Pasadena, California, boasted a Climax Solar Water Heater. But there was a problem. The water heaters were outdoors. At night, when the temperature dropped, the water cooled down.

Day and night

The problem of water heated by day then cooling down at night was solved by another American, William Bailey. In 1909 Bailey invented a new type of solar water heater, which he called the Day and Night Water Heater. It was made up of a solar collector on the roof of the house. Here, water was heated inside pipes. Hot water rose from the collector, along pipes, to a storage tank inside the house. The tank was **insulated** (wrapped with material) to keep the water hot at night.

This modern water heater has been put on the roof of a house, where it will not be in the shade of other buildings or trees.

Bailey's Day and Night Water Heater was soon outselling Kemp's Climax heater. It was a success because people could wash with hot water after a hard day's work and still have hot water for a morning wash.

Modern water heaters

Today, solar water heaters work in a similar way to the Day and Night Water Heater. A modern solar collector is a shallow box with a glass lid. Pipes carry water through the box. Everything in the box is painted black, which helps the pipes to absorb heat.

Setbacks

Just as William Bailey's invention was becoming popular, cheap natural gas became available in the United States. This was soon followed by cheap electricity. These events ruined the market for solar water heaters in the United States for many years.

This diagram shows the parts of a simple solar water heater.

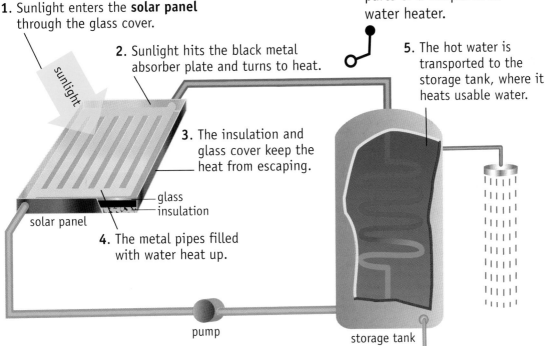

1. Sunlight enters the **solar panel** through the glass cover.

2. Sunlight hits the black metal absorber plate and turns to heat.

3. The insulation and glass cover keep the heat from escaping.

glass
insulation

solar panel

4. The metal pipes filled with water heat up.

pump

5. The hot water is transported to the storage tank, where it heats usable water.

storage tank

water inlet

sunlight

1839—Antoine-César and Alexandre-Edmond Becquerel discover that light can affect the behavior of electricity (see page 14)

SOLAR ELECTRICITY

French scientist Antoine-César Becquerel and his son Alexandre-Edmond were the first people to discover that light can affect electricity. In 1839 the Becquerels found that shining light on the pieces of metal they were using in an experiment changed how easily electricity flowed through the metals.

Some years later, in 1876, English scientist William Grylls Adams discovered that if pieces of the metals selenium and platinum touched each other, and light shone on them, electricity started to flow through the metals. We now call this effect the **photovoltaic** effect.

The very first working **solar cell** was invented around 1886 by the American Charles Fritts. It was made with a piece of the metal selenium coated with a layer of gold. Selenium is a **semiconductor**. It sometimes lets electricity flow through it, and at other times it stops it.

Setbacks

Charles Fritt's solar cell converted only about 1 percent of the solar energy that hit it into electricity. It didn't produce enough electricity to be useful for anything. And the selenium and gold it used were also very expensive. However, it did show that solar cells were possible.

Practical solar cells

It was another 70 years before practical solar cells were invented. The breakthrough was made in 1953 at the AT&T Bell Laboratories in Murray Hill, New Jersey. It was the work of a team of scientists who worked at the laboratories. They were Gerald Pearson, Daryl Chapin, and Calvin Fuller (from left to right in the photograph below).

The Bell Laboratories

The Bell Laboratories were research laboratories opened in 1925 by the American Telephone and Telegraph Company (AT&T). Scientists and engineers there made many groundbreaking inventions. Examples include one of the first digital computers (1937), the **transistor** (1947), and the first telecommunications **satellite**, *Telstar* (1960s).

Silicon solar cells

The team at the Bell Laboratories discovered that a solar cell could be made from another type of semiconductor material, called **silicon**. They used two types of silicon, called *n-type* and *p-type*, touching each other. When light shone on the junction (joining point) between the two pieces of silicon, the cell made an electric current.

A solar cell is made up of layers of different semiconductor materials.

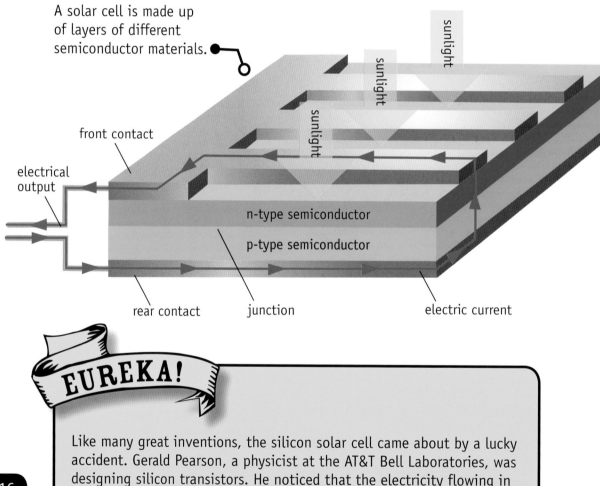

sunlight

sunlight

sunlight

front contact

electrical output

n-type semiconductor

p-type semiconductor

rear contact

junction

electric current

EUREKA!

Like many great inventions, the silicon solar cell came about by a lucky accident. Gerald Pearson, a physicist at the AT&T Bell Laboratories, was designing silicon transistors. He noticed that the electricity flowing in the transistors changed when light shone on them.

1876—William Grylls Adams discovers that selenium and platinum together can turn light into electricity (see page 14)

1865   1870   1875

More electricity

This new type of cell produced six times more electricity from light than the original selenium solar cells invented by Charles Fritts (see page 14). This was a huge improvement. The Bell Laboratories team also figured out how to **manufacture** (make) their solar cells in large numbers.

In 1957 a solar-powered toy called the "Do Nothing Machine" was created.

around 1886—Charles Fritts invents the first solar cell, using selenium (see page 14)

SOLAR POWER IN SPACE

The new **silicon solar cells** were great, but hardly anybody bought them. They were extremely expensive to make. Nobody could afford them except the U.S. military.

The U.S. military was also developing its first experimental space **satellite**. Solar power was an obvious technology for satellites, as batteries could never be replaced in space. But the U.S. Navy, which was designing the satellite, thought that solar cells were too new and untested. Then satellite expert Dr Hans Ziegler persuaded the Navy to use solar cells as well as batteries. The satellite, called *Vanguard I*, was launched in 1958. It was an important moment for the history of solar power.

This is *Vanguard I*, the first solar-powered satellite.

1890s—Clarence Kemp introduces his Climax Solar Water Heater (see page 11)

The batteries on board *Vanguard I* failed after just a few days in space. But the satellite was rescued by its solar cells. They kept the satellite's radio transmitters working for six years, before it was finally switched off.

Cheaper solar cells

In the 1970s, Elliot Berman invented a much cheaper way to make solar cells. He used low-quality silicon. Each cell cost just one-fifth as much as previous cells. The new cell was used in beacons at sea and lighthouses. Companies making gadgets such as watches and calculators also began putting solar cells on their machines.

This is one of the first watches with a solar cell, made in 1976.

19

1909—William Bailey introduces his Day and Night Water Heater (see page 12)

In the 1980s, engineers built the first **solar power stations**. A solar power station makes large amounts of electricity, just like other types of power stations (such as coal-fired power stations). There are two types of solar power station: **photovoltaic** power stations and **solar thermal** power stations.

Solar thermal power

Solar thermal power stations capture solar energy and use it to boil water to make steam. The steam drives **turbines** that power electricity **generators**. The first thermal power station was Solar One in California, completed in 1981.

Setbacks

The problem with solar power is that it is unable to produce power at night, when there is no sunlight, and power is reduced when it is cloudy. Other sources of power are always needed as a backup.

20

At Solar One, hundreds of mirrors focused sunlight onto a central tower.

1925—The AT&T Bell Laboratories are founded in New York City (see page 15)

This solar thermal power station collects sunlight in troughs, which then heat oil in pipes.

Photovoltaic power

Photovoltaic power stations use **solar cells** to produce electricity from sunlight. The first photovoltaic power station to supply electricity to homes was built in Hesperia, California, in 1982. The solar cells swiveled (spun around) on posts to face the Sun all day, collecting the greatest possible amount of light.

Setbacks

In the 1970s there was a world oil-supply crisis. The price of oil rose dramatically, so many people became interested in alternative (different) energy sources, such as solar energy. But in the 1980s, the price of oil fell again. People went back to using oil, and some early solar power stations had to be shut down.

By the 1980s, **solar cells** were good enough and cheap enough to allow inventors to experiment with solar-powered cars. The idea was simple, but it was not easy to put into practice. The problem was fitting enough **solar panels** onto a car to produce enough electricity to make the car go.

The very first solar-powered car, the *Quiet Achiever*, was designed by Danish inventor Hans Tholstrup in 1982. In December 1982, Tholstrup drove his car more than 4,000 kilometers (2,485 miles) across Australia.

Solar Challenges

In 1987 Tholstrup started a race for solar-powered cars called the World Solar Challenge. Cars have to cross Australia from north to south, covering 3,021 kilometers (1,877 miles). The race is meant to encourage research into solar-powered transportation. In 2007 Louis Palmer from Switzerland drove his normal-sized solar car, *Solartaxi*, around the world. This showed that solar cars are a practical idea.

Here, two solar-powered cars are taking part in the 2009 World Solar Challenge.

22

Hans Tholstrup (born 1945)

Hans Tholstrup was born and grew up in Denmark, but he later moved to Australia. He became interested in bikes and cars at an early age. Throughout his life, he has gone on many adventures in vehicles and set many records, including the first solo flight around the world without navigation equipment (1973). He also made the fastest motorcycle trip around the world (1974). Tholstrup became interested in **renewable energy** in the 1970s, before inventing his solar car.

23

1953—Gerald Pearson, Daryl Chapin, and Calvin Fuller invent the first **silicon** solar cell (see page 15)

1958—The U.S. *Vanguard I* **satellite** is launched, carrying solar cells to produce its electricity (see page 18)

Solar-powered planes

Solar-powered airplanes suffer from the same problems as solar-powered cars. Solar-powered planes can only go slowly through the air, because of the small amount of electricity being produced to power the motors. The plane needs long, wide wings to fit the solar panels onto and lift it into the air. The first **unmanned** solar-powered aircraft was invented in 1974 by Roland Boucher. It was called *AstroFlight Sunrise*.

Solar Challenger

The first person-carrying solar plane was *Gossamer Penguin*, designed by Paul MacCready. It made many short flights in 1980. An improved plane designed by MacCready, *Solar Challenger*, crossed the English Channel in 1981, powered by 16,000 solar panels. Remote-controlled solar-powered planes include NASA's *Pathfinder* (1994) and *Helios* (1999). These were designed for researching Earth's surface from above. In 2001 *Helios* flew at a world-record altitude of 29,523 meters (96,860 feet).

Here, the *Solar Challenger* aircraft is being prepared for a flight in 1980.

1970s—Elliot Berman finds a way to make cheap silicon solar cells (see page 19). An oil supply crisis makes oil very expensive, leading to research into solar power (see page 21).

1974—The first solar-powered plane, *AstroFlight Sunrise*, takes to the air

1975—The first solar-powered boat is launched

1965   1970   1975

Q
↳ *Planet Solar* is designed to sail around the world on solar energy.

Setbacks

NASA's *Helios* solar-powered aircraft was destroyed when it fell into the sea in 2003. The plane flew into very turbulent air, which bent its lightweight wing so far that it snapped. This put an end to NASA's solar-plane experiments.

Solar-powered boats

The first solar-powered boat was designed in 1975. It had solar cells that powered an electric motor, which turned its propeller. Small solar-powered boats are now common.

1981—The first **solar thermal** power station, Solar One, is opened (see page 20). *Solar Challenger* flies across the English Channel.

1982—Hans Tholstrup builds the first solar car, *Quiet Achiever*, and drives it 2,485 miles across Australia (see page 22). The first **photovoltaic** power station is opened (see page 21).

1987— The first World Solar Challenge takes place in Australia (see page 22)

Today, we use solar power in more and more places. Some of the examples you have probably seen are solar-powered watches, calculators, yard lights, and water heaters. Less well-known examples include solar-powered lighthouses, water-well pumps, railroad signals, parking meters, and solar ovens.

Solar buildings

Many modern buildings have **solar cells** that provide electricity for the building. The cells are built into the structure and are known as building-integrated **photovoltaics** (BIPVs). One person to thank for this development is Subhendu Guha, who invented roof tiles that contain solar cells. These are called solar shingles. Many new homes include solar heating systems.

Solar cells on roofs have come a long way since early water heaters and bulky **solar panels**.

1994—NASA's *Pathfinder* remote-controlled solar plane flies for the first time (see page 24)

1996—Subhendu Guha invents solar shingles

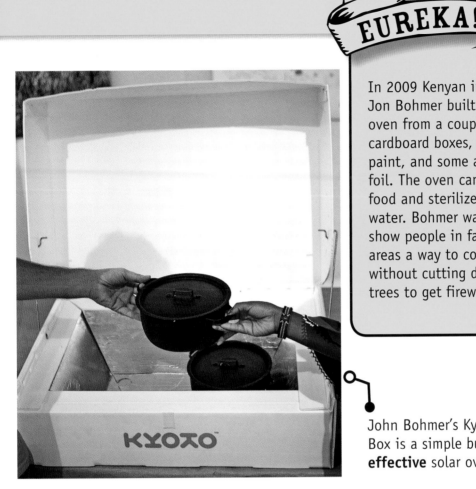

In 2009 Kenyan inventor Jon Bohmer built a solar oven from a couple of cardboard boxes, black paint, and some aluminum foil. The oven can cook food and sterilize (clean) water. Bohmer wanted to show people in faraway areas a way to cook without cutting down trees to get firewood.

John Bohmer's Kyoto Box is a simple but **effective** solar oven.

Solar cells and the planet

Solar cells are one of the most **environmentally friendly** inventions ever. They are an important technology in fighting **global warming**. Machines that are powered by solar cells do not have batteries that have to be replaced, and they do not use electricity that is made at **fossil-fuel**-burning power stations. We are well on the way to having practical solar-powered cars, which do not produce harmful gases like carbon monoxide.

27

2003—NASA's *Helios* solar-powered plane crashes (see page 25)

2007—The *Sun 21* boat crosses the Atlantic Ocean using solar power alone

2009—Jon Bohmer invents a simple solar oven for use in remote areas of the world

TIMELINE

around 400 BCE
From Greek writings, we know that the ancient Greeks built solar-heated houses

200 BCE
The Greek scientist Archimedes may have sunk a Roman fleet using sunlight and mirrors

around 1200 CE
The Pueblo people build solar-heated terraced houses in the town of Acoma, New Mexico

1909
William Bailey introduces his Day and Night Water Heater

1890s
Clarence Kemp introduces his Climax Solar Water Heater

around 1886
Charles Fritts invents the first **solar cell**, using selenium

1925
The AT&T Bell Laboratories are founded in New York City

1953
Gerald Pearson, Daryl Chapin, and Calvin Fuller invent the first **silicon** solar cell

1958
The U.S. *Vanguard I* **satellite** is launched, carrying solar cells to produce its electricity

1982
Hans Tholstrup builds the first solar car, *Quiet Achiever*, and drives it 4,000 kilometers (2,485 miles) across Australia

1982
The first **photovoltaic** power station is opened

1987
The first World Solar Challenge takes place in Australia

1994
NASA's *Pathfinder* remote-controlled solar plane flies for the first time

1996
Subhendu Guha invents solar shingles

around 1700
"Saltbox" houses are built by settlers in New England

1767
Horace de Saussure invents the first **solar collector**, or "hot box"

1800s
Sun rooms and greenhouses become increasingly popular in northern Europe

1876
William Grylls Adams discovers that selenium and platinum together can turn light into electricity

1839
Antoine-César and Alexandre-Edmond Becquerel discover that light can affect the behavior of electricity

1970s
Elliot Berman finds a way to make cheap silicon solar cells

1970s
An oil supply crisis makes oil very expensive, leading to research into solar power

1974
The first solar-powered plane, *AstroFlight Sunrise*, takes to the air

1981
Solar Challenger flies across the English Channel

1981
The first **solar thermal** power station, Solar One, is opened in California

1975
The first solar-powered boat is launched

2003
NASA's *Helios* solar-powered plane crashes

2007
The *Sun 21* boat crosses the Atlantic Ocean using solar power alone

2009
Jon Bohmer invents a simple solar oven for use in remote areas of the world

GLOSSARY

absorb soak up. For example, how a sponge soaks up water.

climate usual weather conditions in a region

effective working well

environmentally friendly not harmful to the environment

fossil fuel fuel that is made from the remains of ancient plants and animals, such as oil, gas, and, coal

generator device that makes electricity when its central part (called a rotor) is spun around

global warming gradual warming of Earth's atmosphere caused mainly by gases released when we burn certain fuels

humidity amount of moisture that is in the air

insulated wrapped so that heat cannot easily escape

manufacture make something in large numbers

northern hemisphere half of Earth north of the equator (an imaginary line around the middle of Earth)

photovoltaic effect of something that creates electricity when it is hit by light

renewable energy natural source of energy that will never run out, such as solar energy or wind energy

satellite spacecraft that moves around Earth again and again

semiconductor material that sometimes lets electricity flow through it, and sometimes stops electricity from flowing

silicon common material found in sand that is used to make semiconductors

solar cell electronic device that turns sunlight into electricity

solar collector device that traps solar energy and uses it to heat a liquid, such as water, or to cook food

solar panel panel that contains several solar cells that produce electricity, or a panel that contains a solar collector

solar power station power station that produces electricity from solar energy

solar thermal describes technology that traps the heat of the Sun

transistor device made of semiconductor material that can turn an electrical current on or off

turbine revolving motor driven by the flow of water, steam, or gas, which is used to drive a generator to produce electricity

unmanned not having a person onboard

FIND OUT MORE

Books

Morris, Neil. *Solar Power* (*Energy Sources*). Mankato, Minn.: Smart Apple Media, 2010.

Oxlade, Chris. *Inventors' Secret Scrapbook* (*Crabtree Connections*). New York: Crabtree, 2011.

Rooney, Anne. *Solar Power* (*Energy for the Future and Global Warming*). Pleasantville, N.Y.: Gareth Stevens, 2008.

Websites

www.eia.doe.gov/kids/energy.cfm?page=solar_home-basics
There is lots of information about solar power on this U.S. Energy Information Administration website.

www.solarenergy.org/younger-kids
This Solar Energy International website answers many questions about solar power.

www.worldsolarchallenge.org
This is the official website of the World Solar Challenge, the solar-powered car race from one end of Australia to the other.

Places to visit

The Museum of Science, Boston
1 Science Park
Boston, Massachusetts 02114
www.mos.org

The Museum of Science and Industry
57th Street and Lake Shore Drive
Chicago, Illinois 60637
www.msichicago.org

INDEX